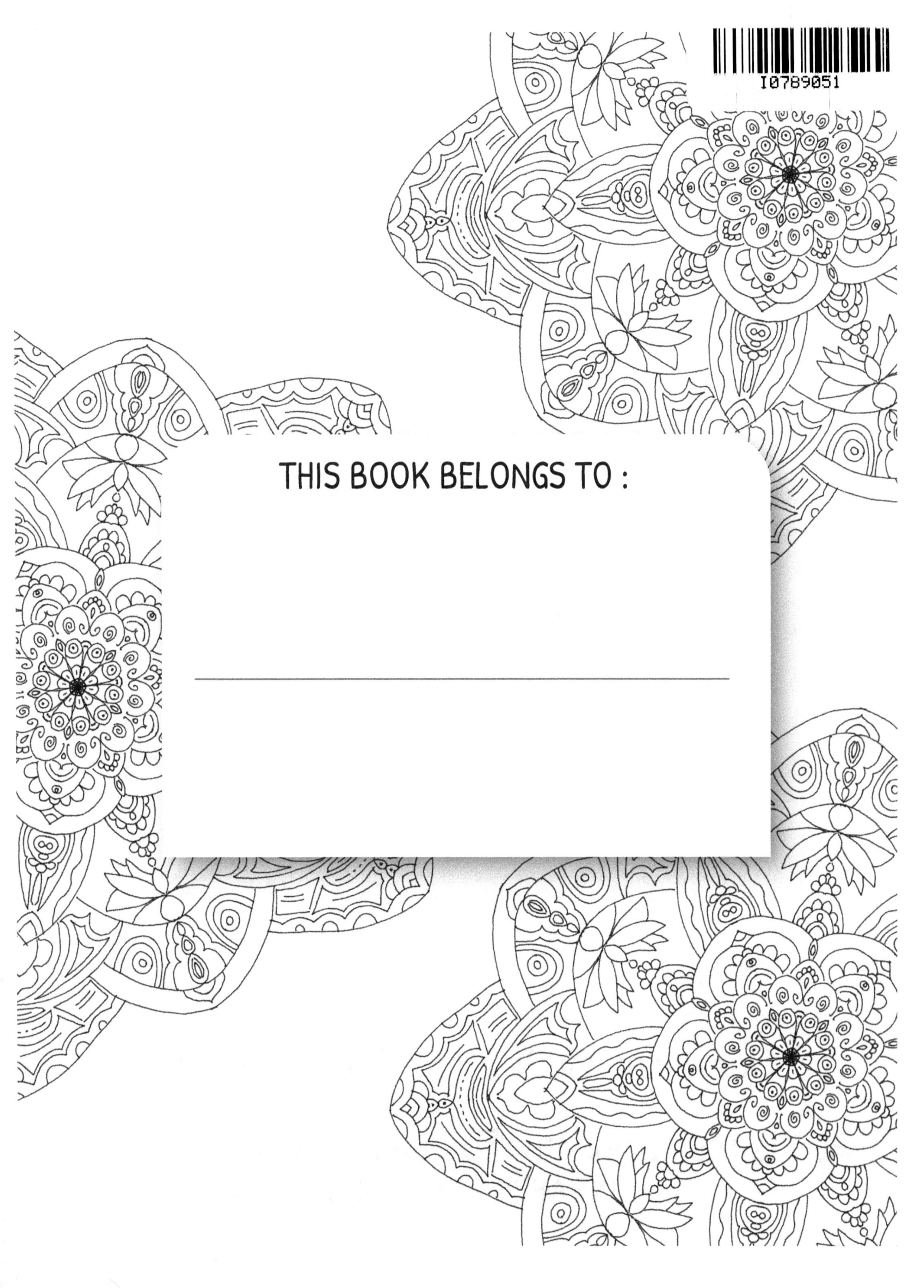
THIS BOOK BELONGS TO :

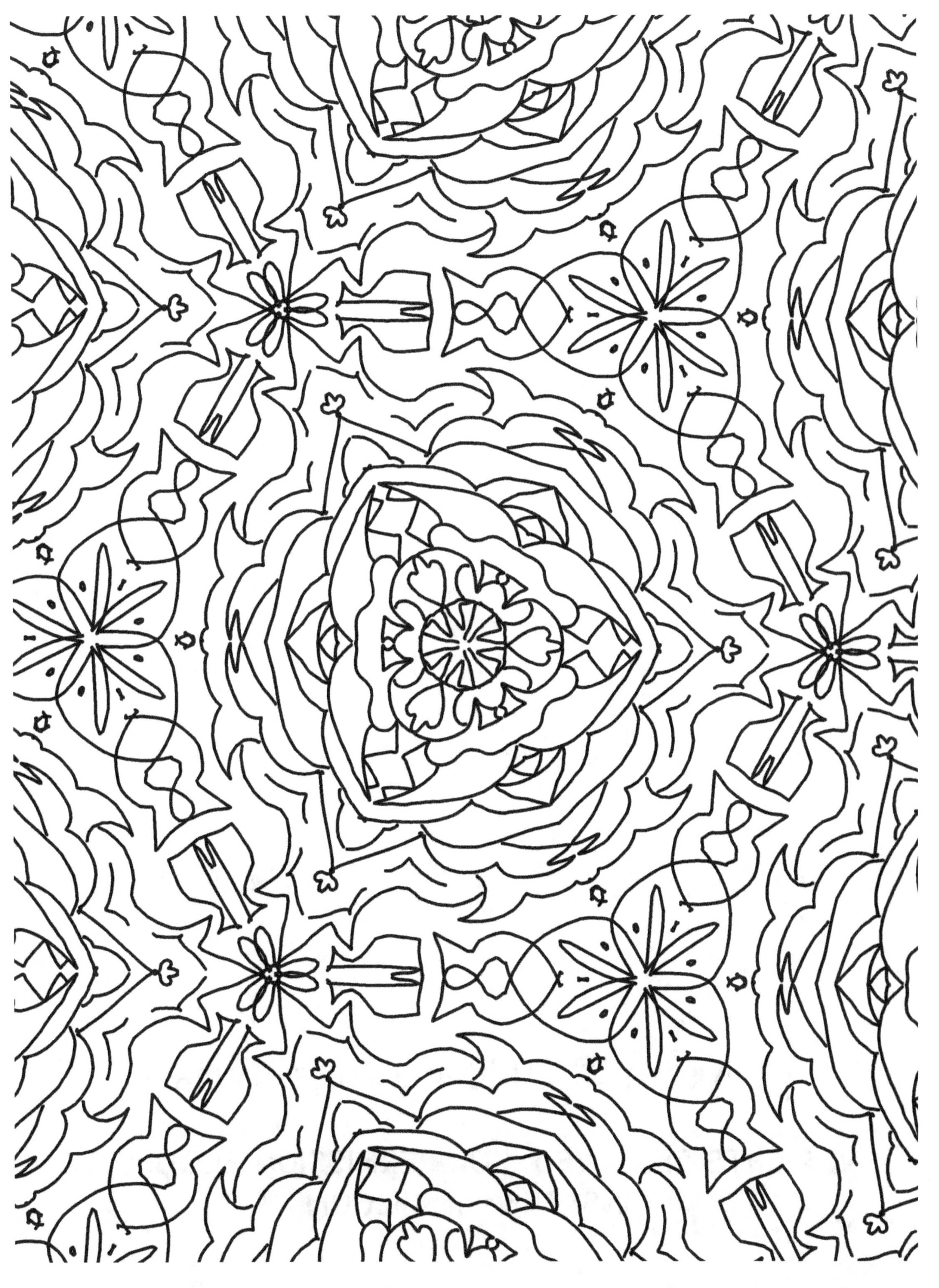

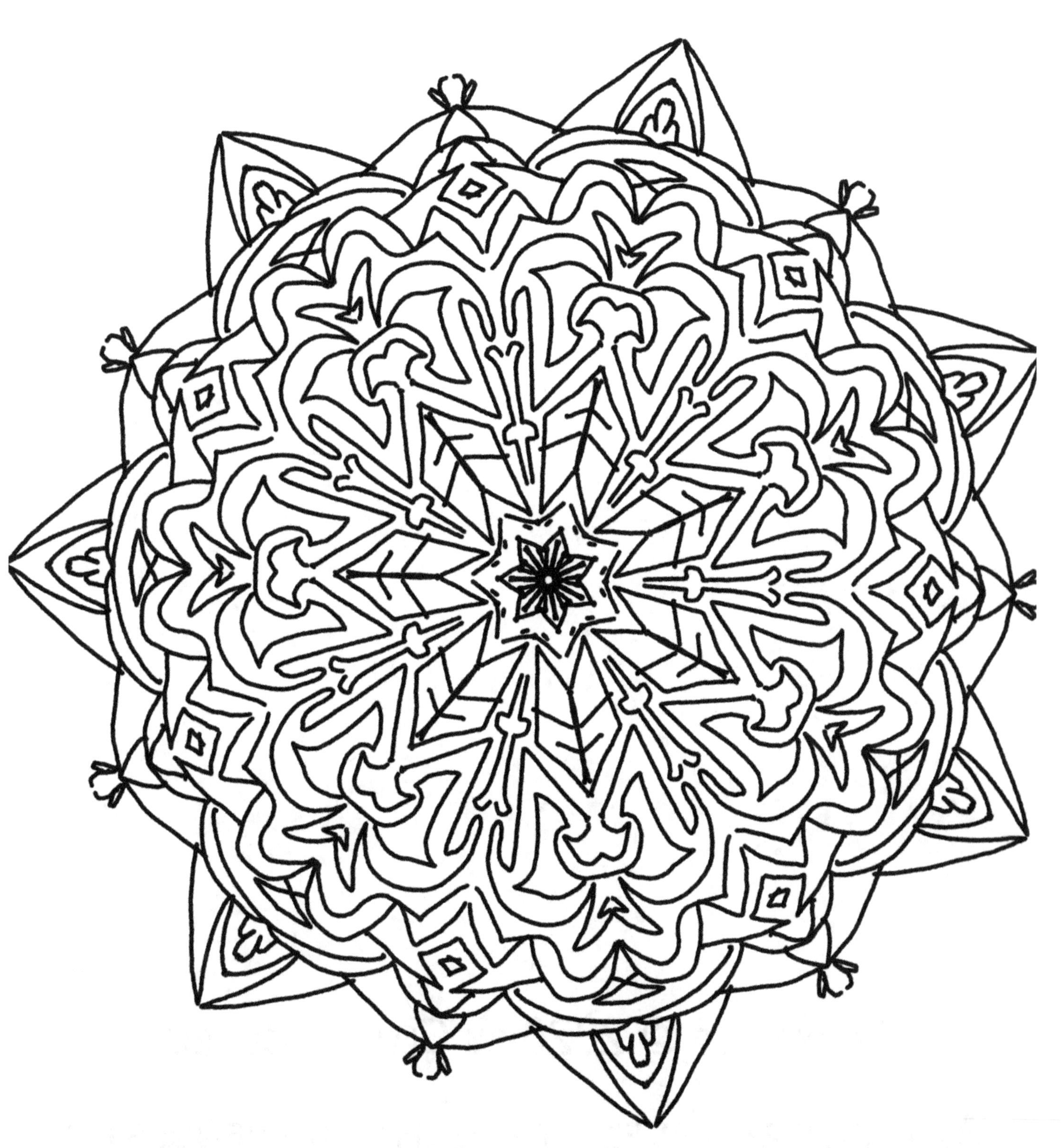

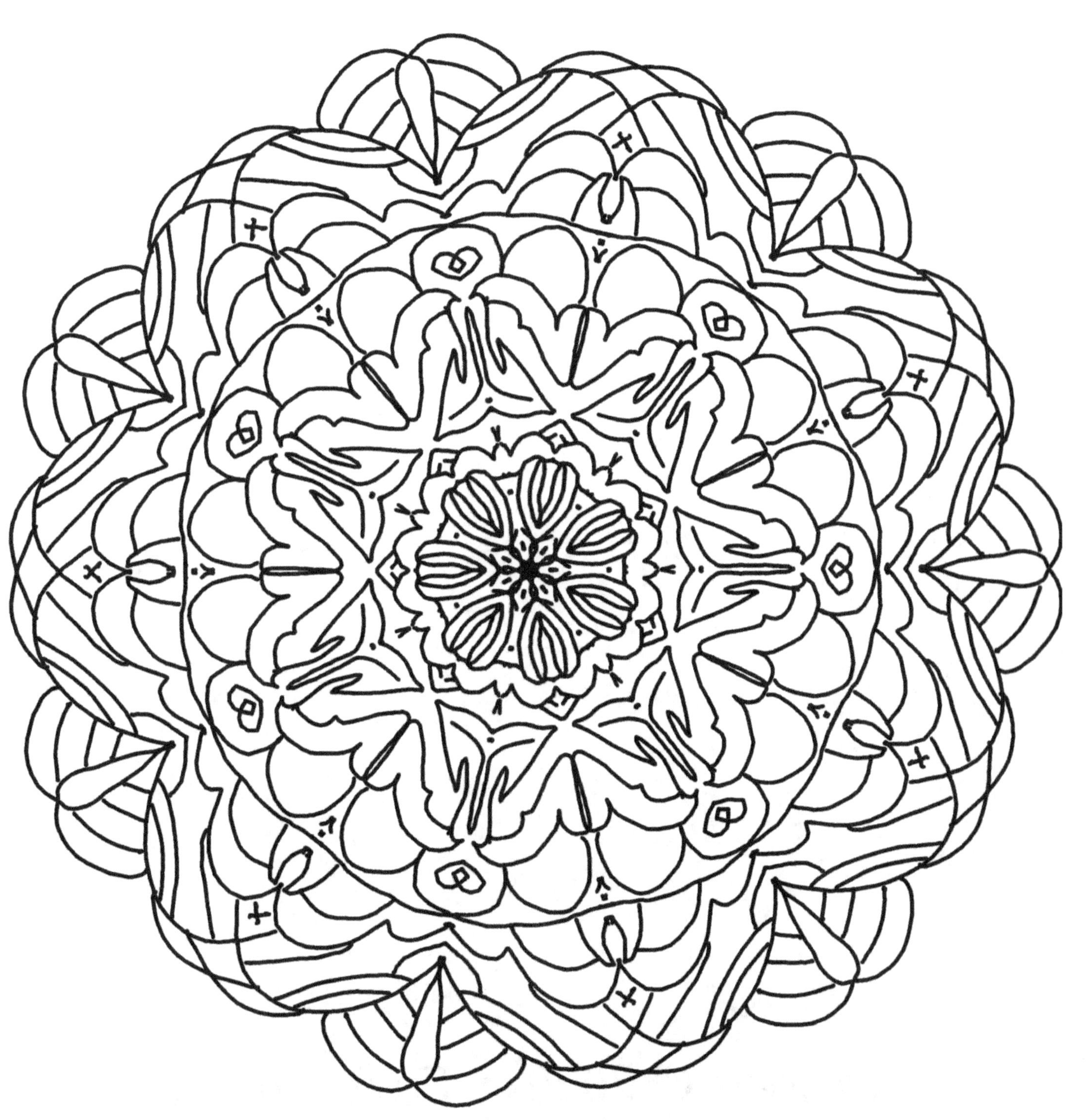

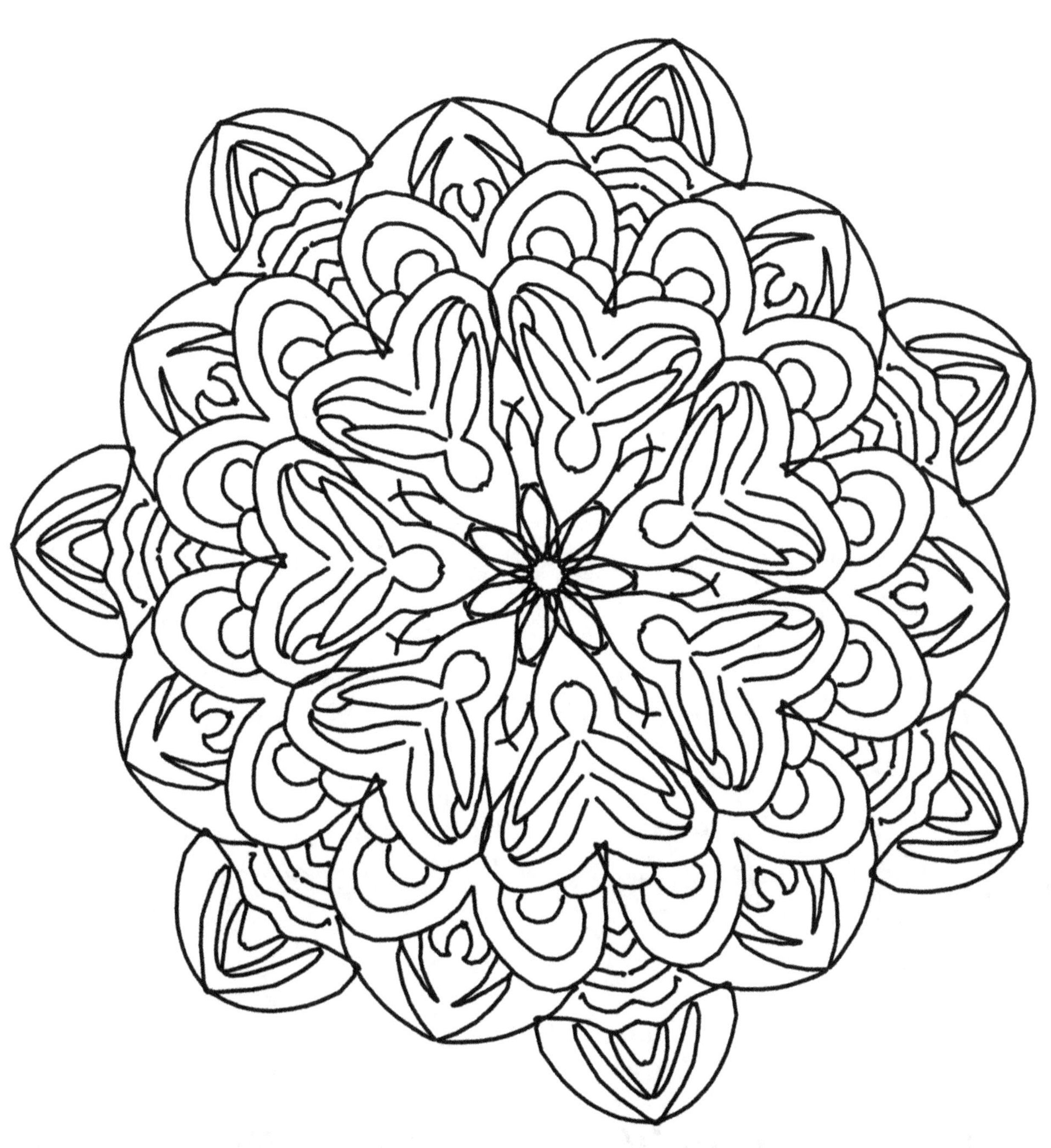

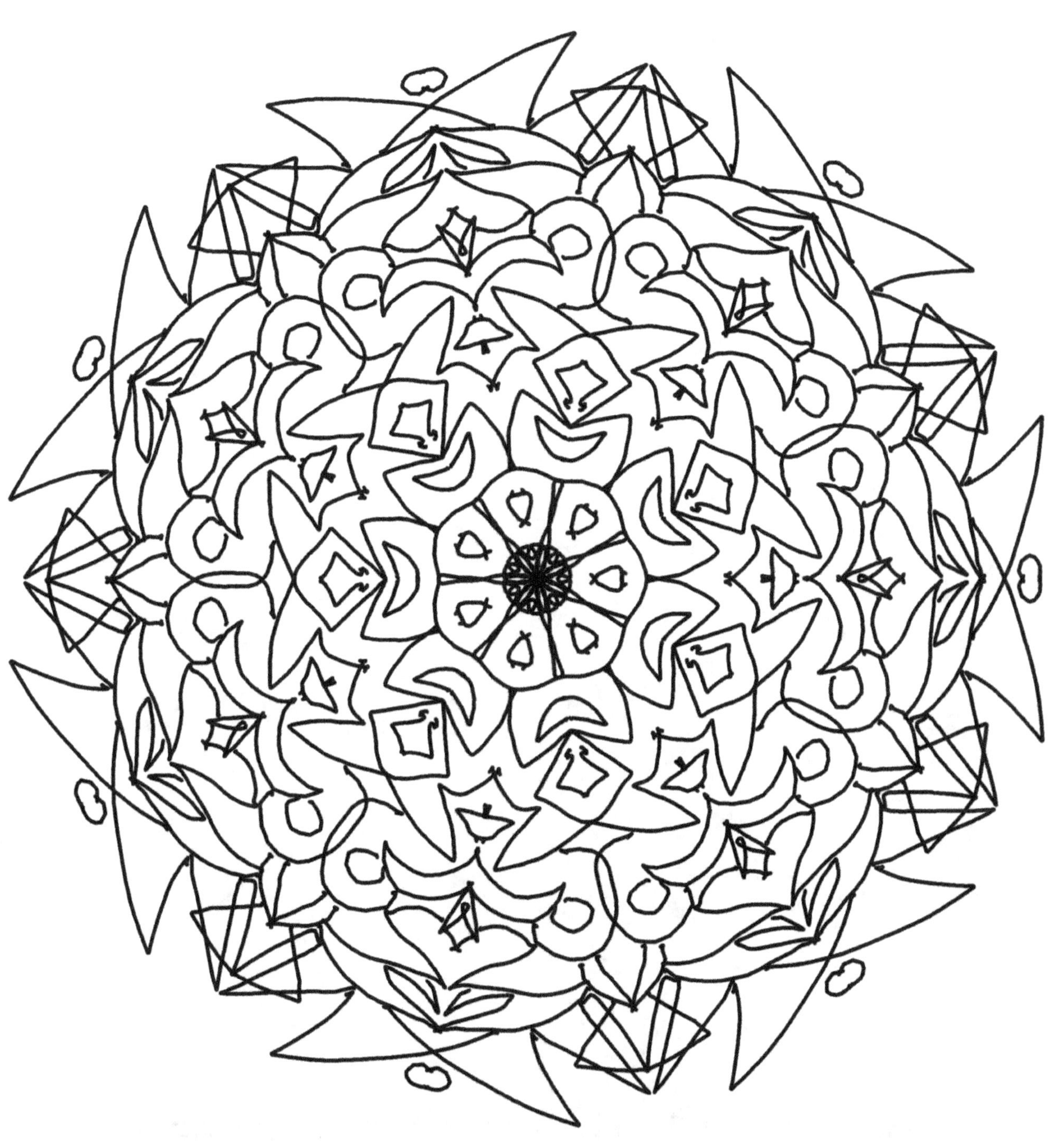

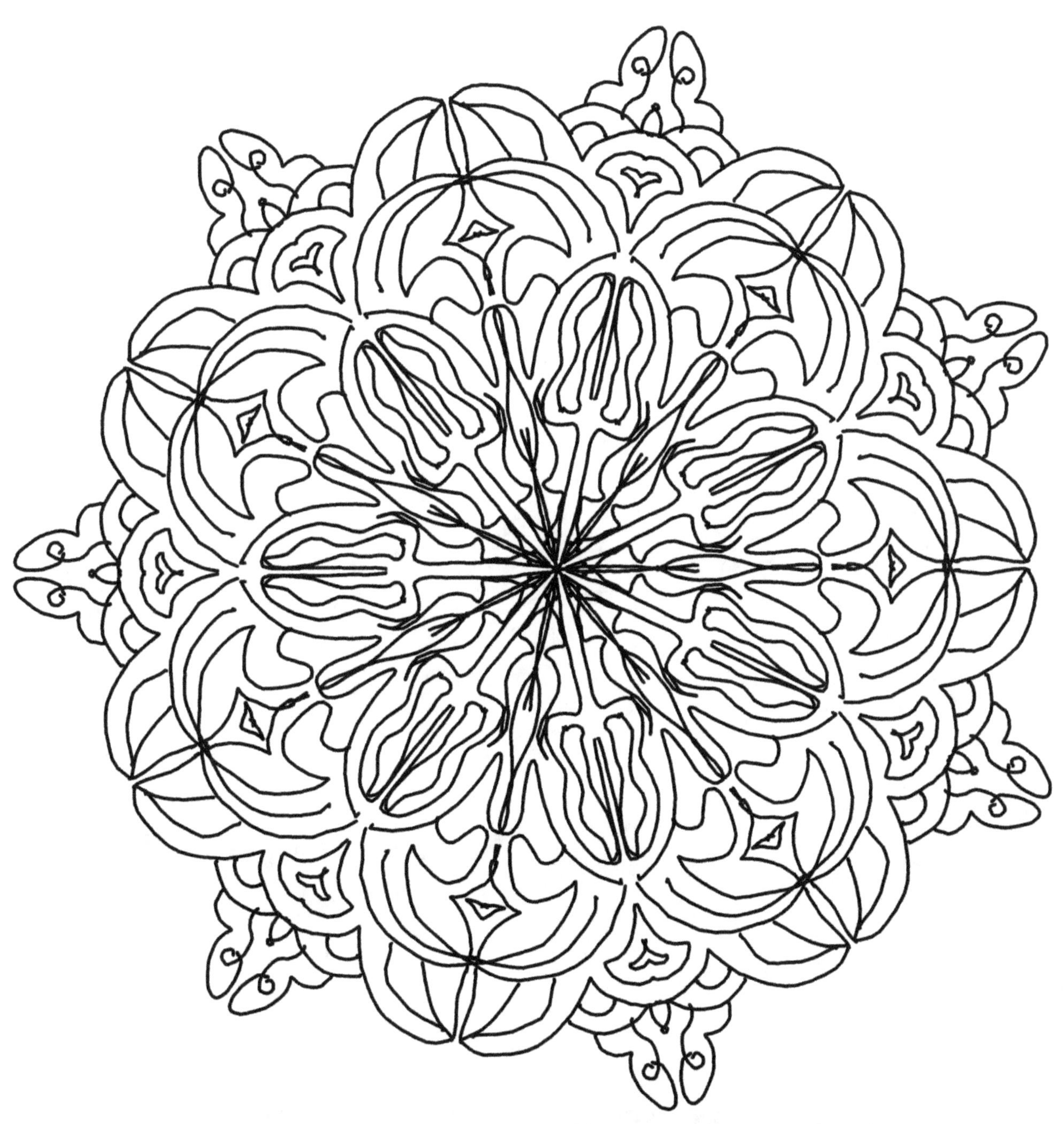

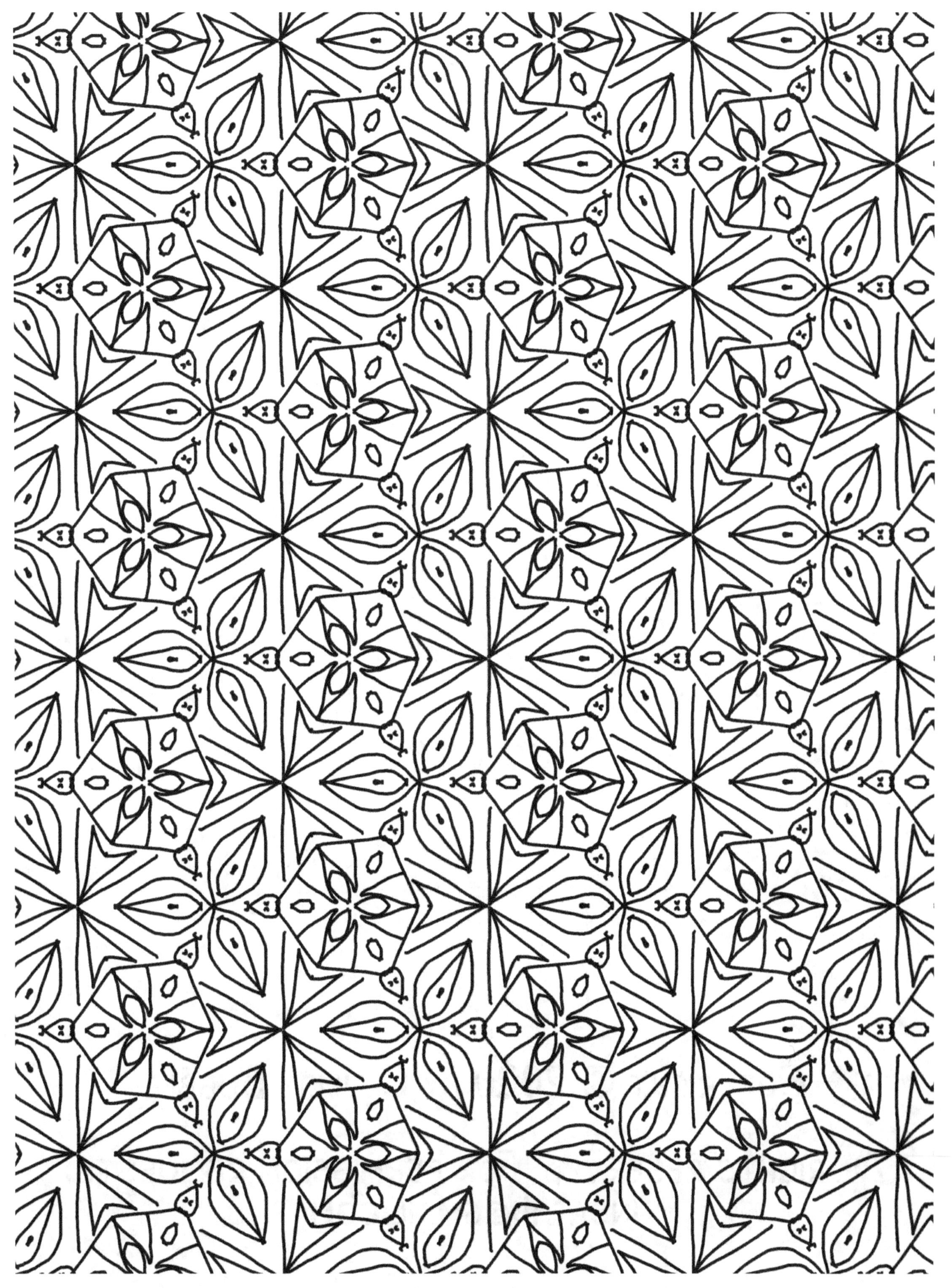

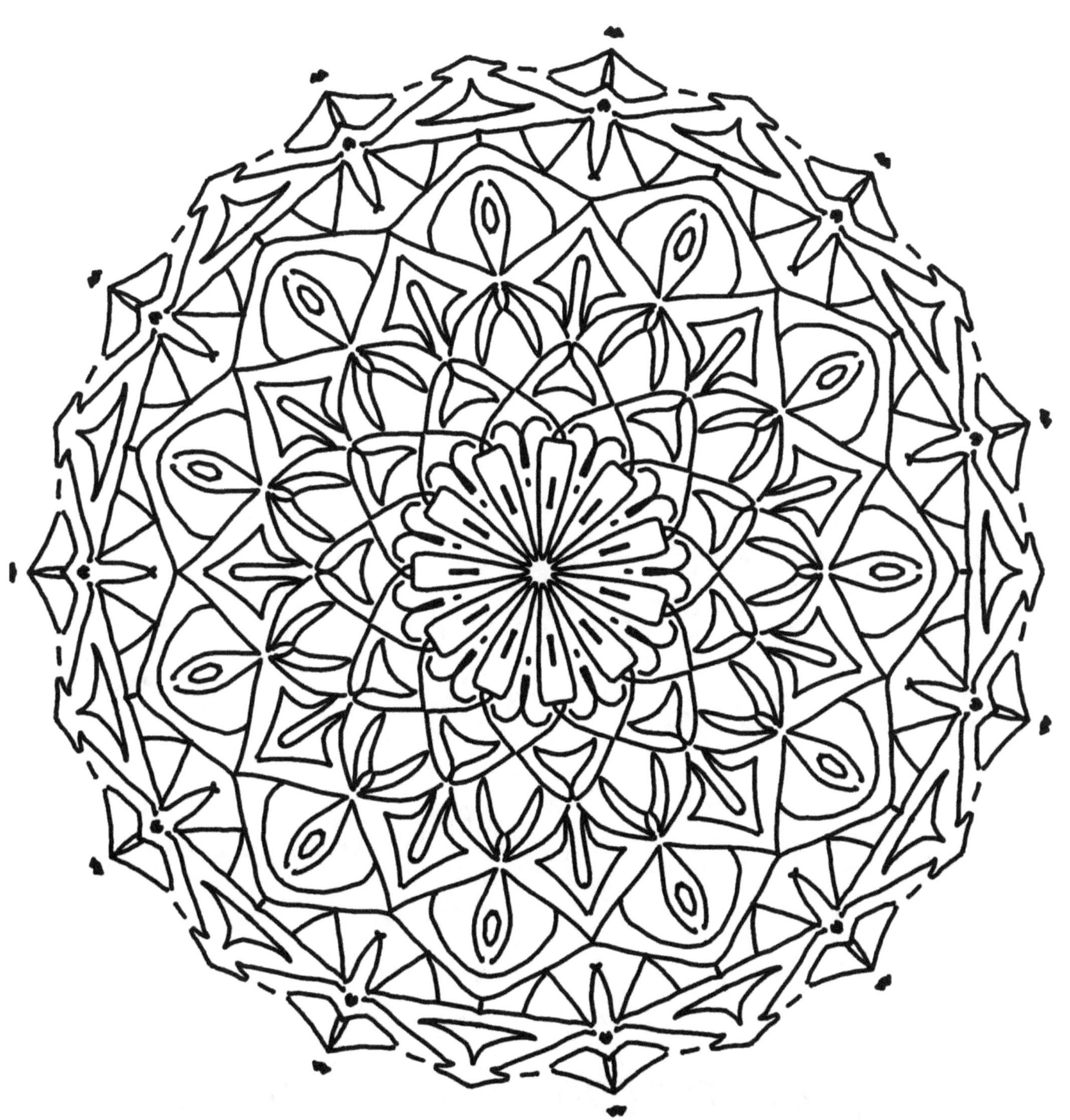

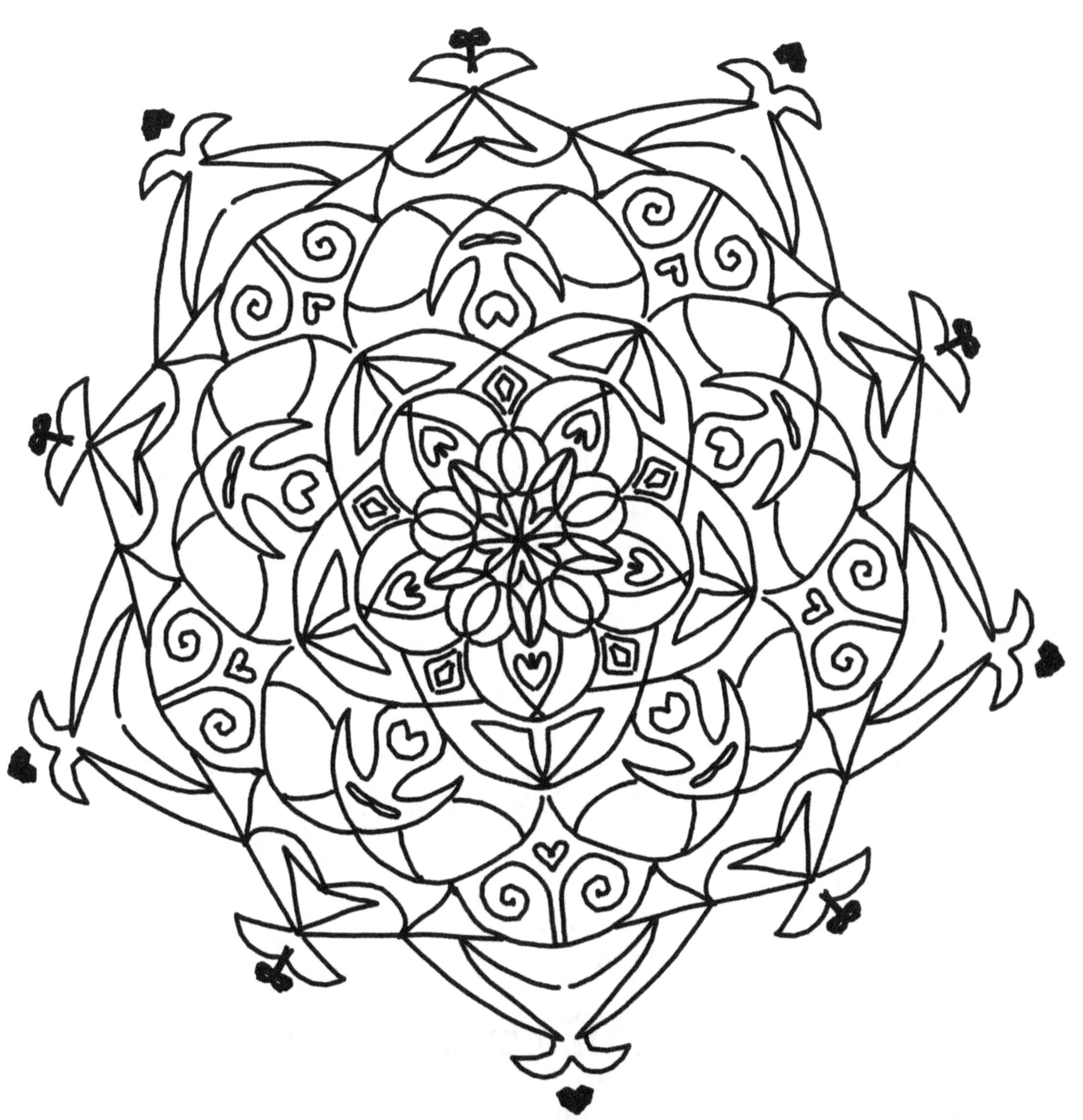

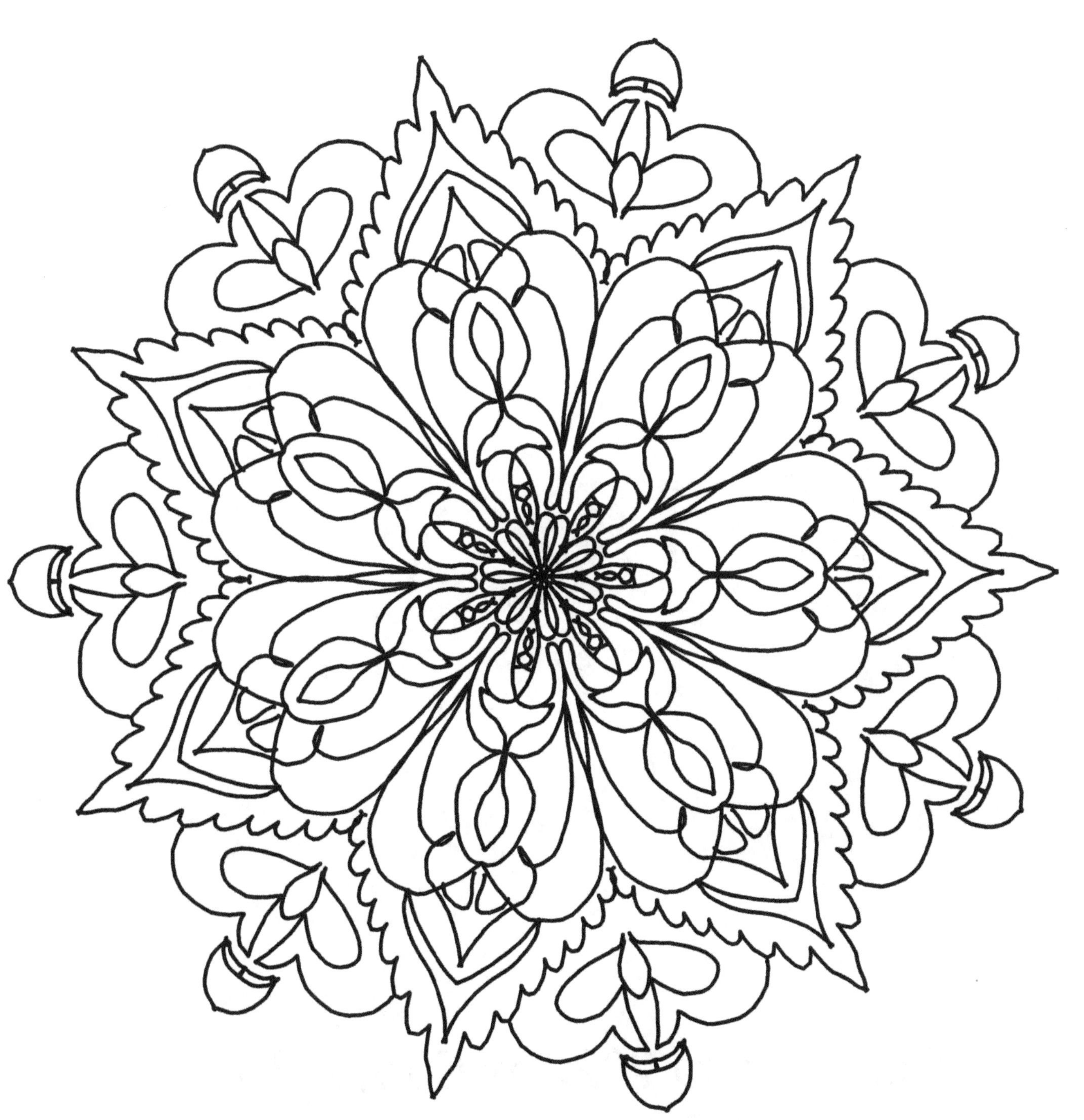

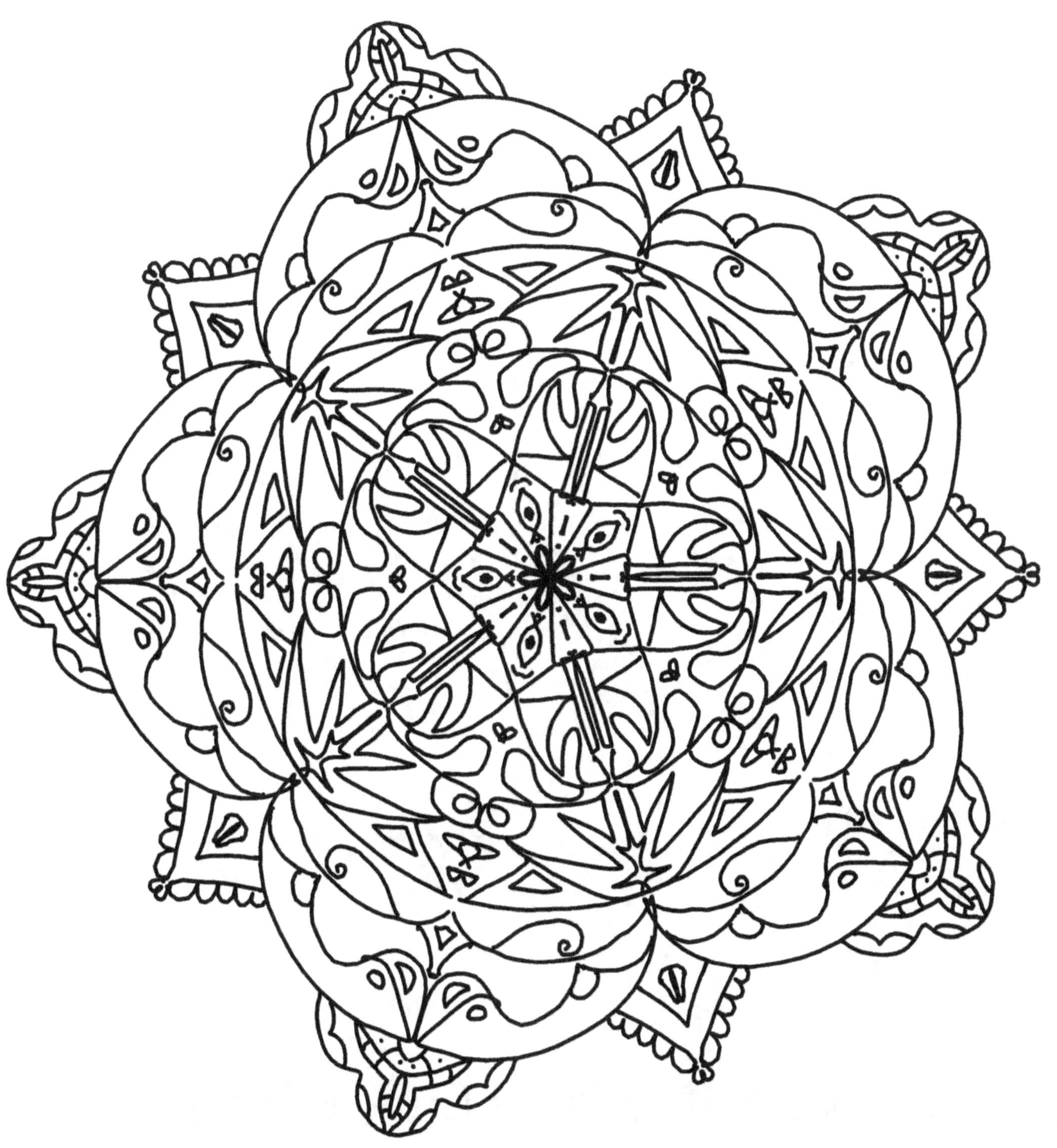

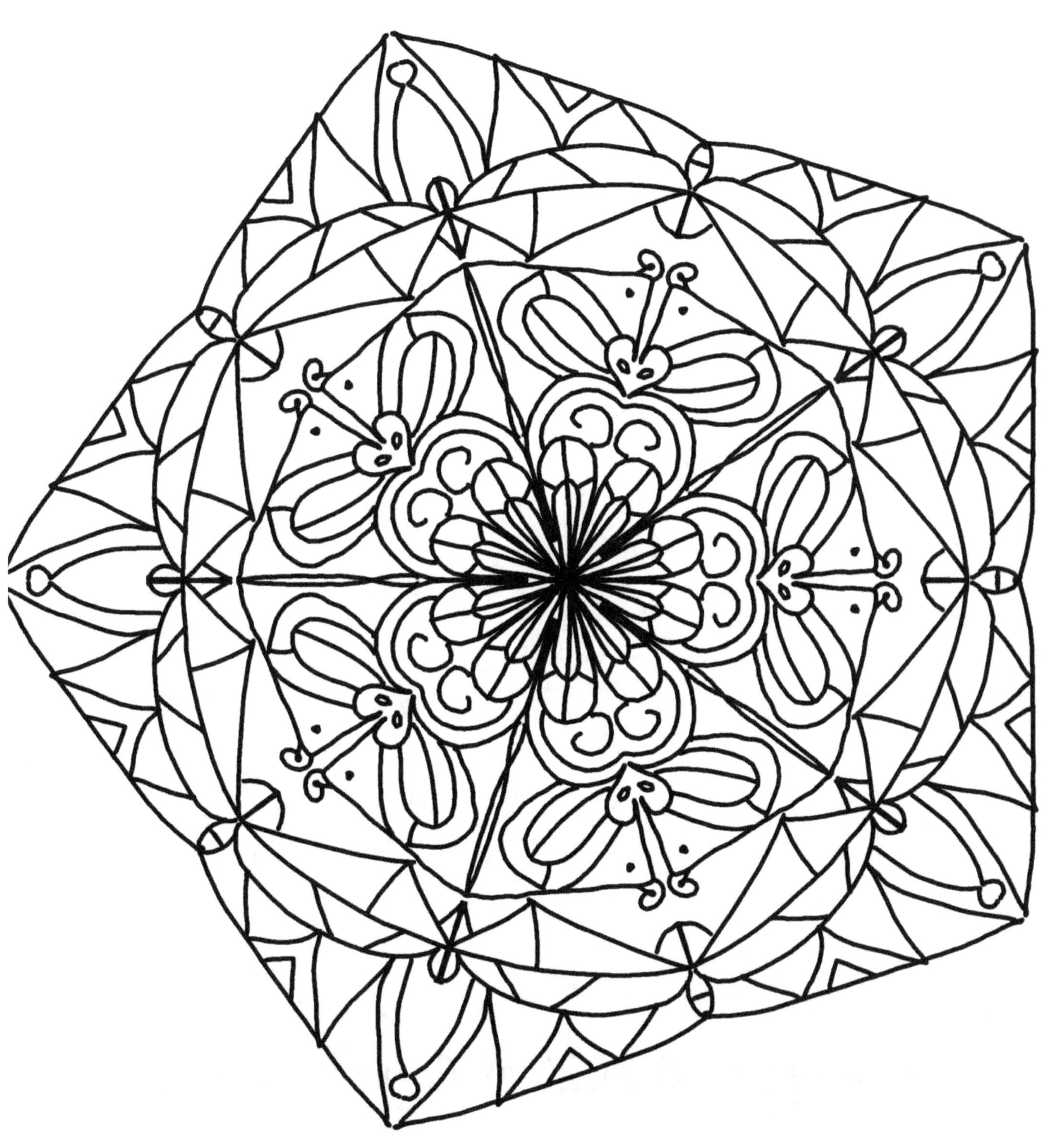

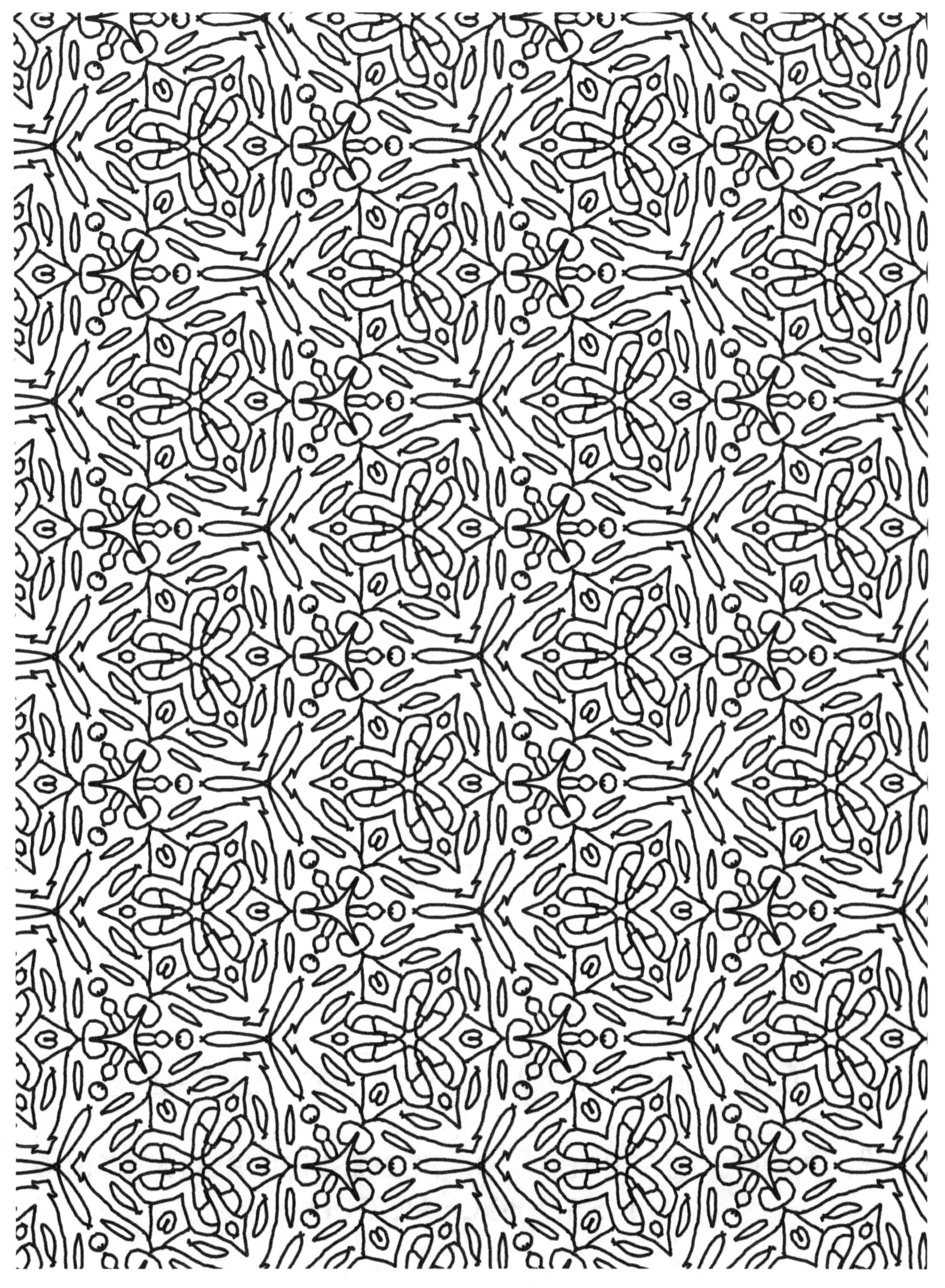

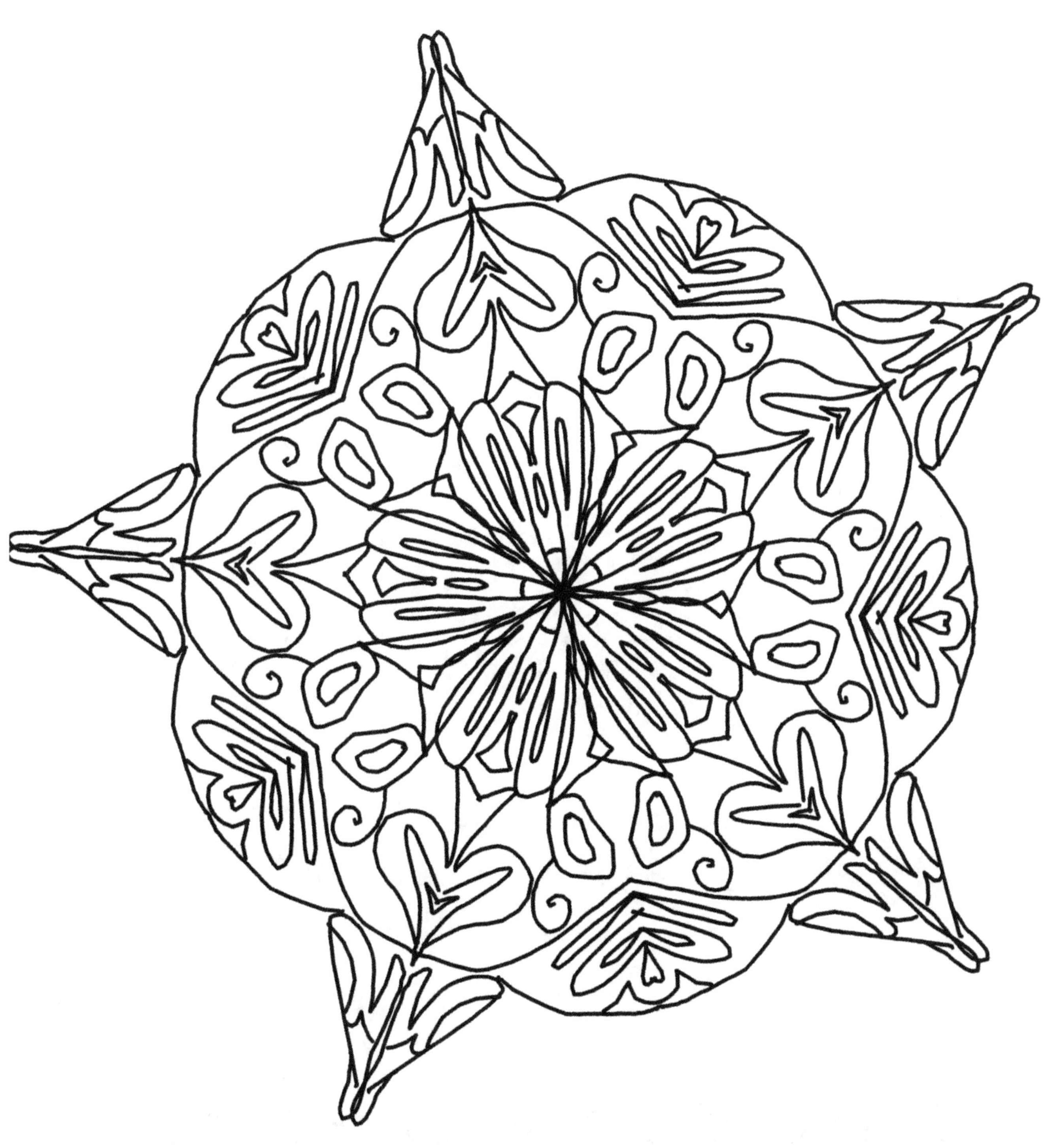

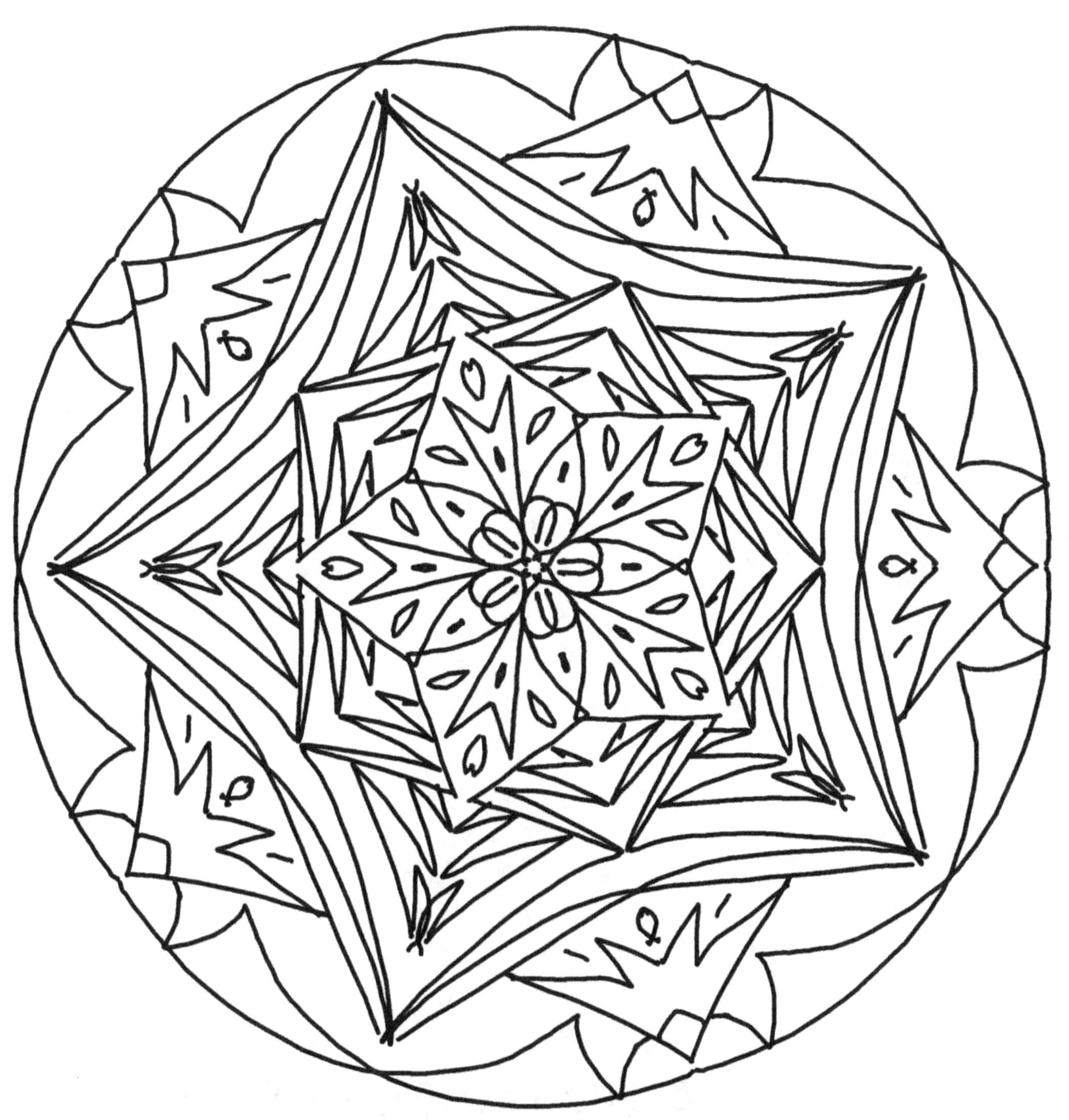

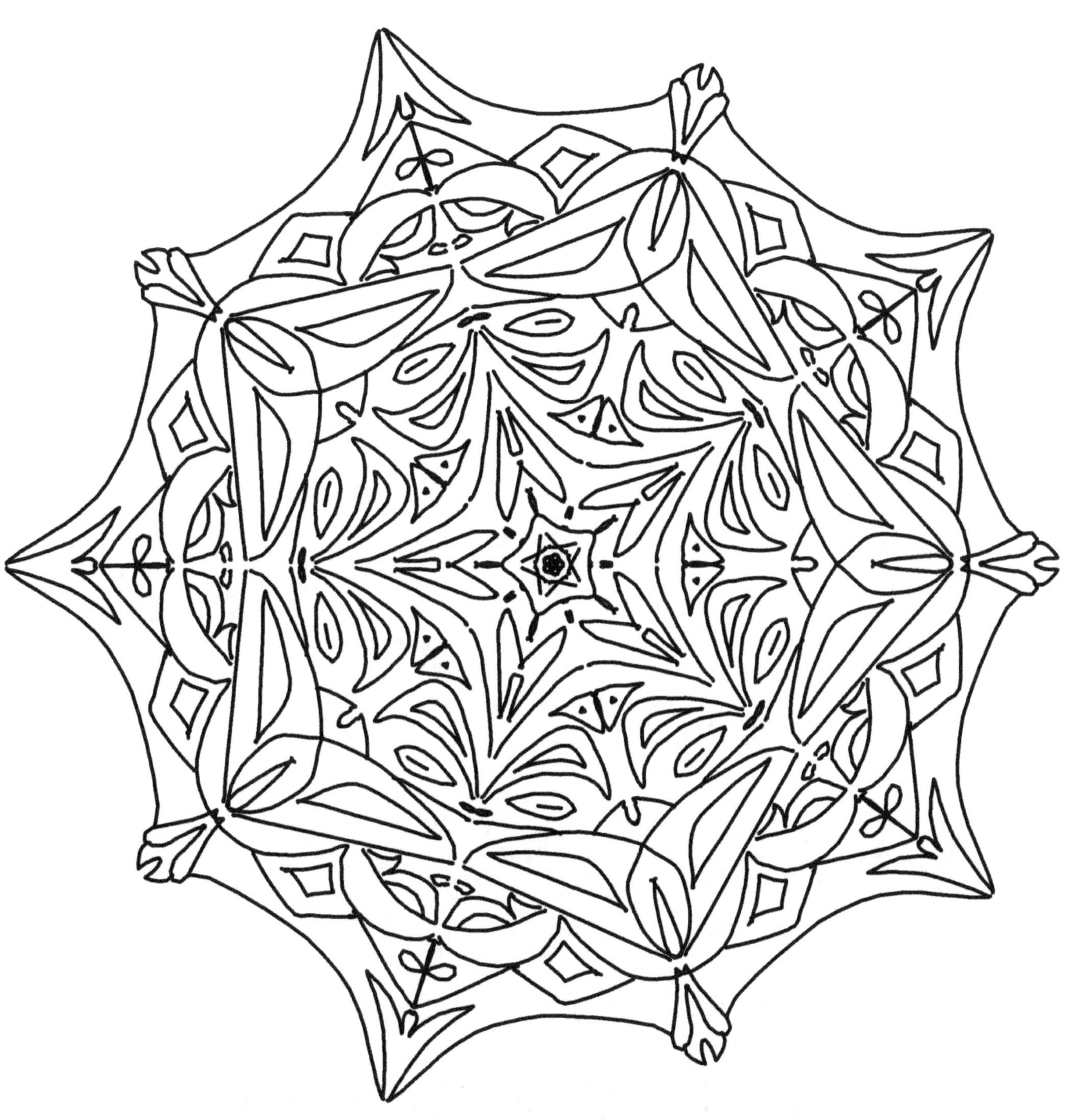

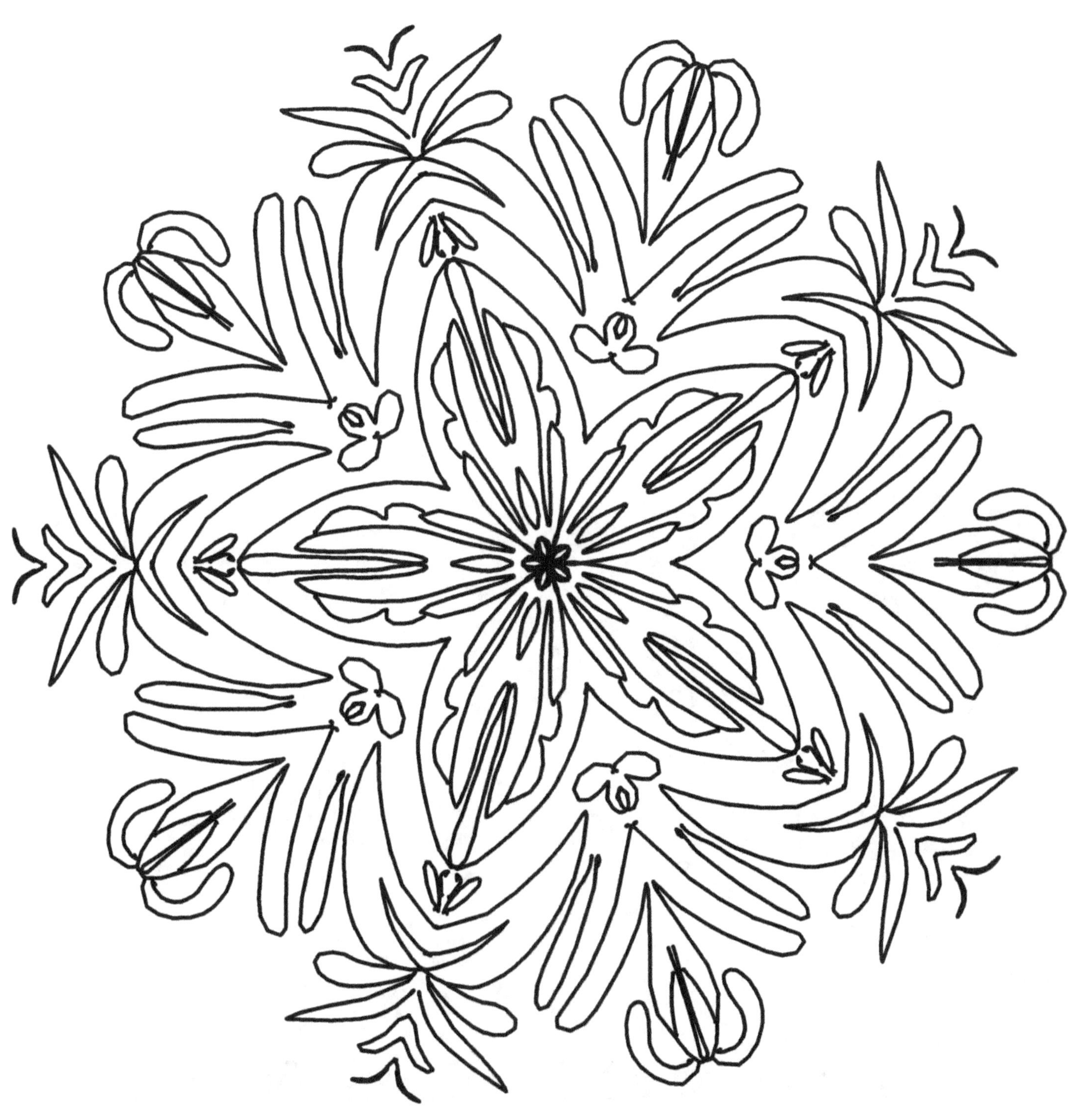

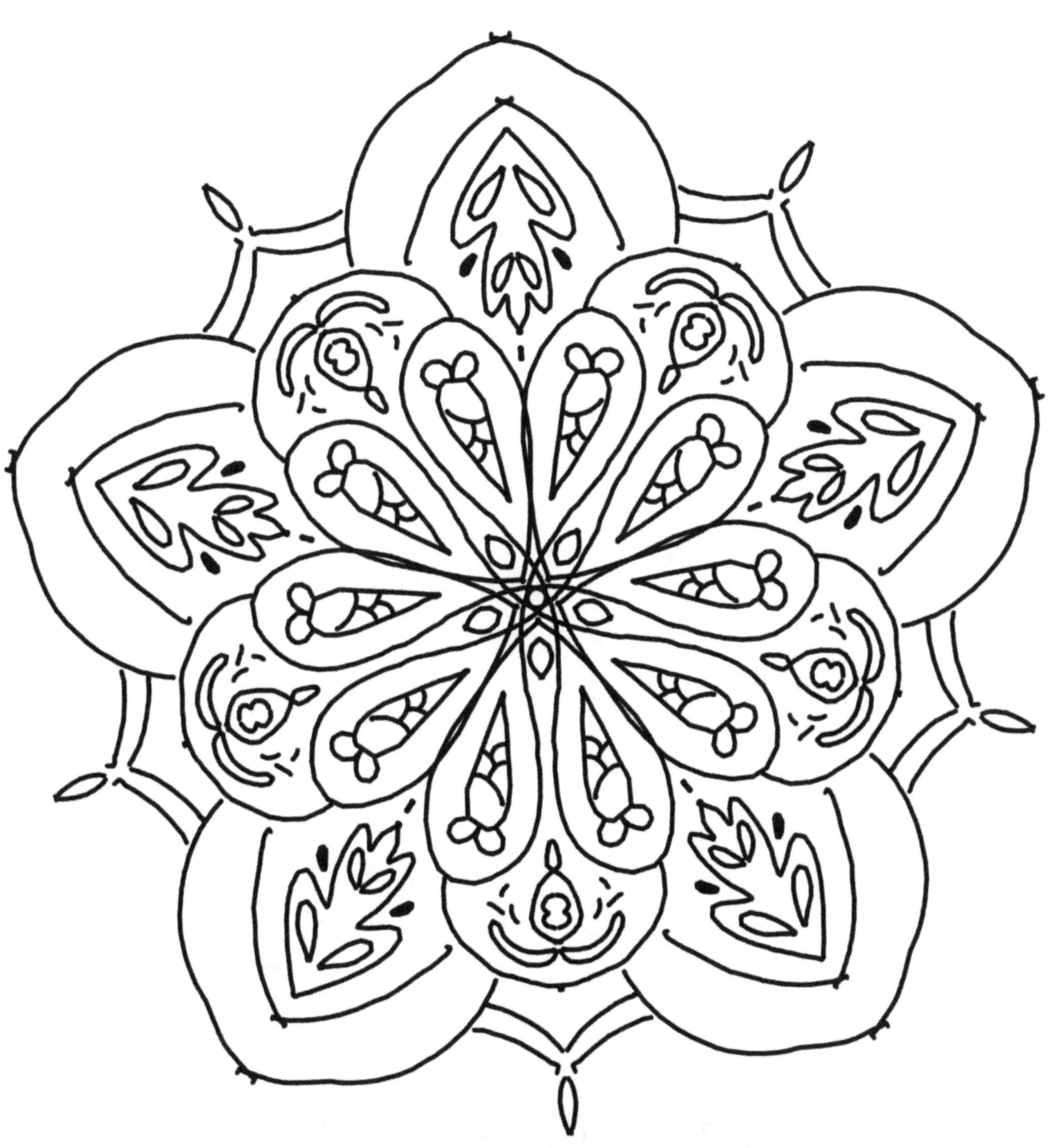

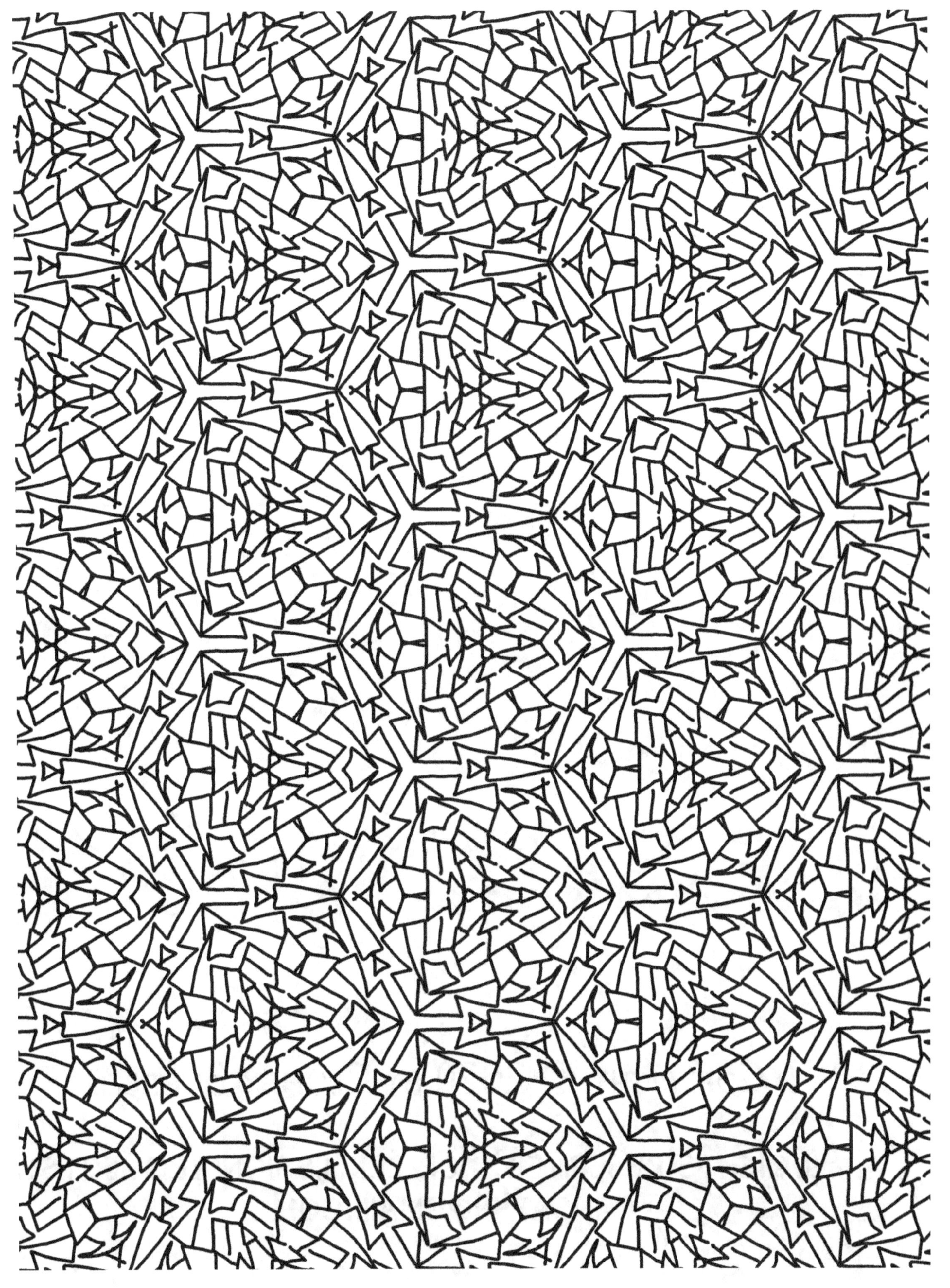

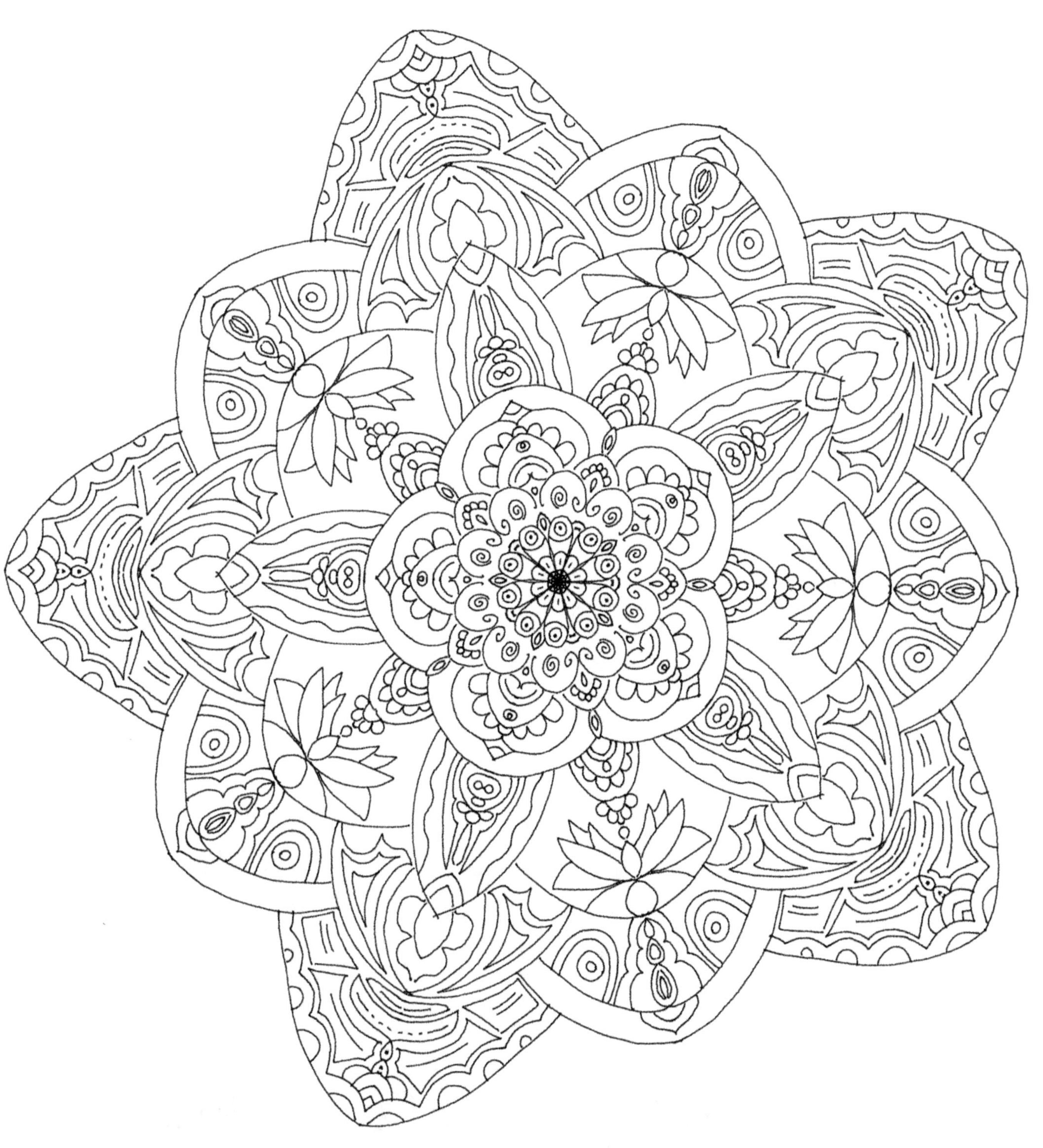

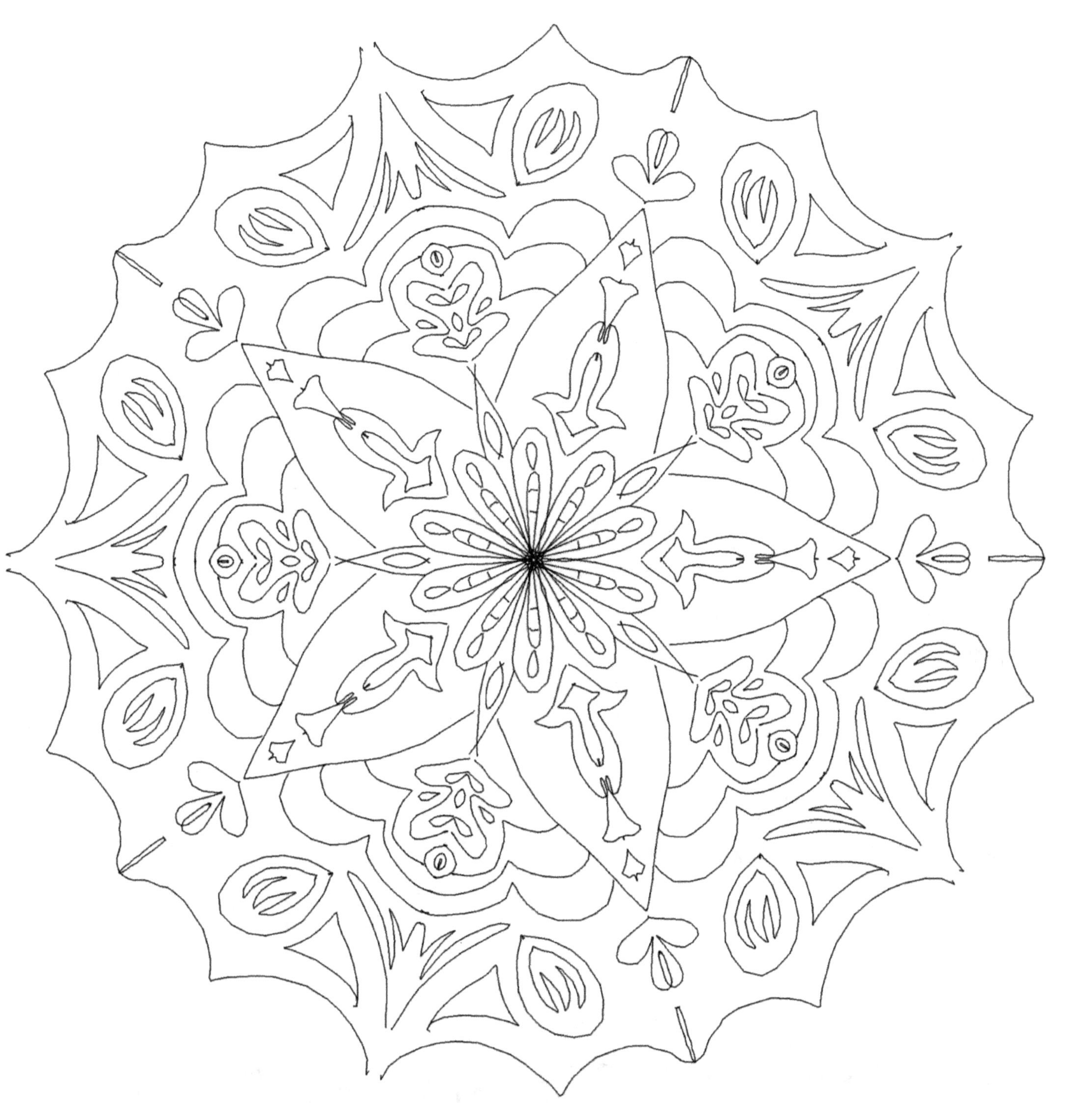

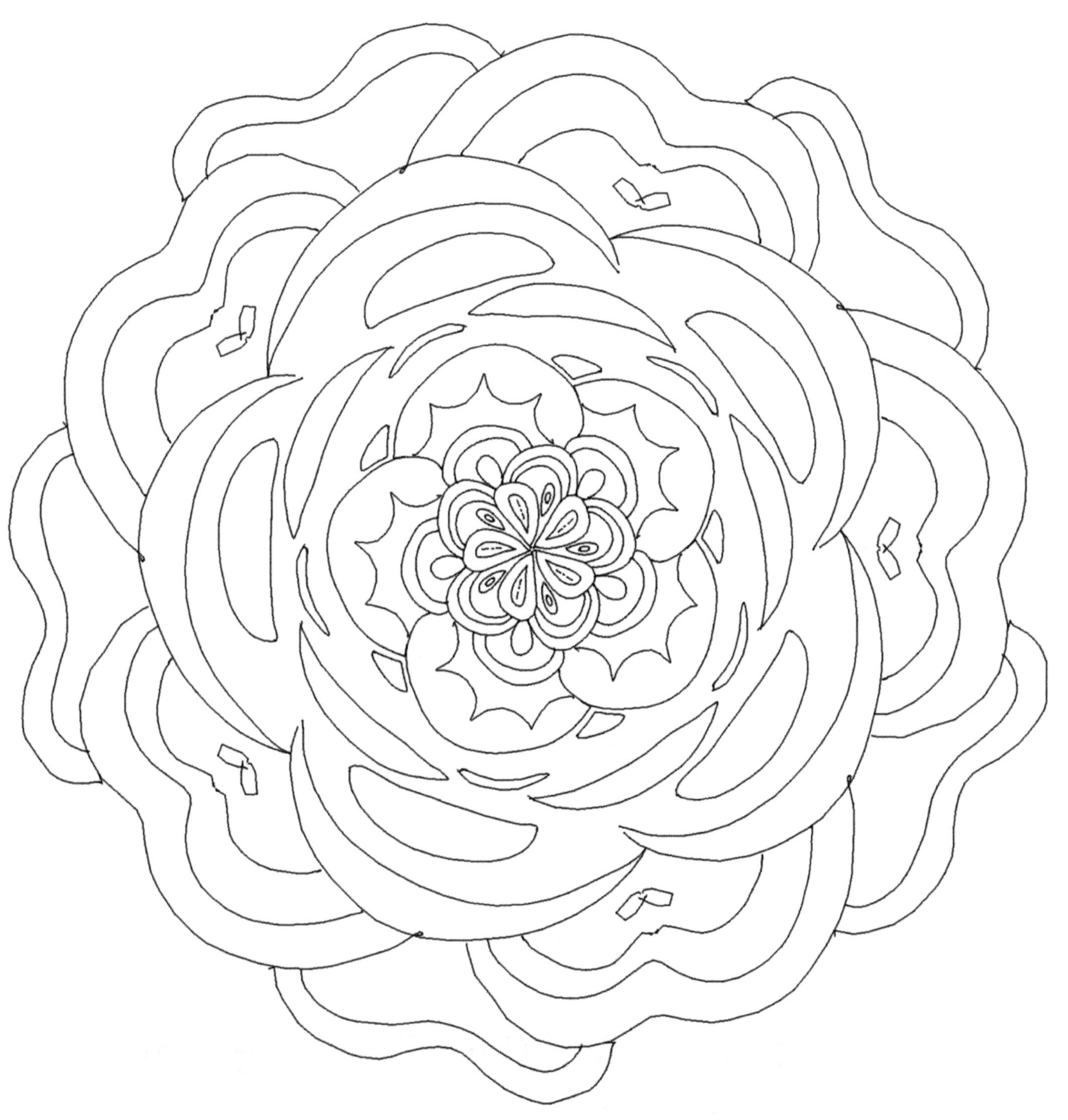

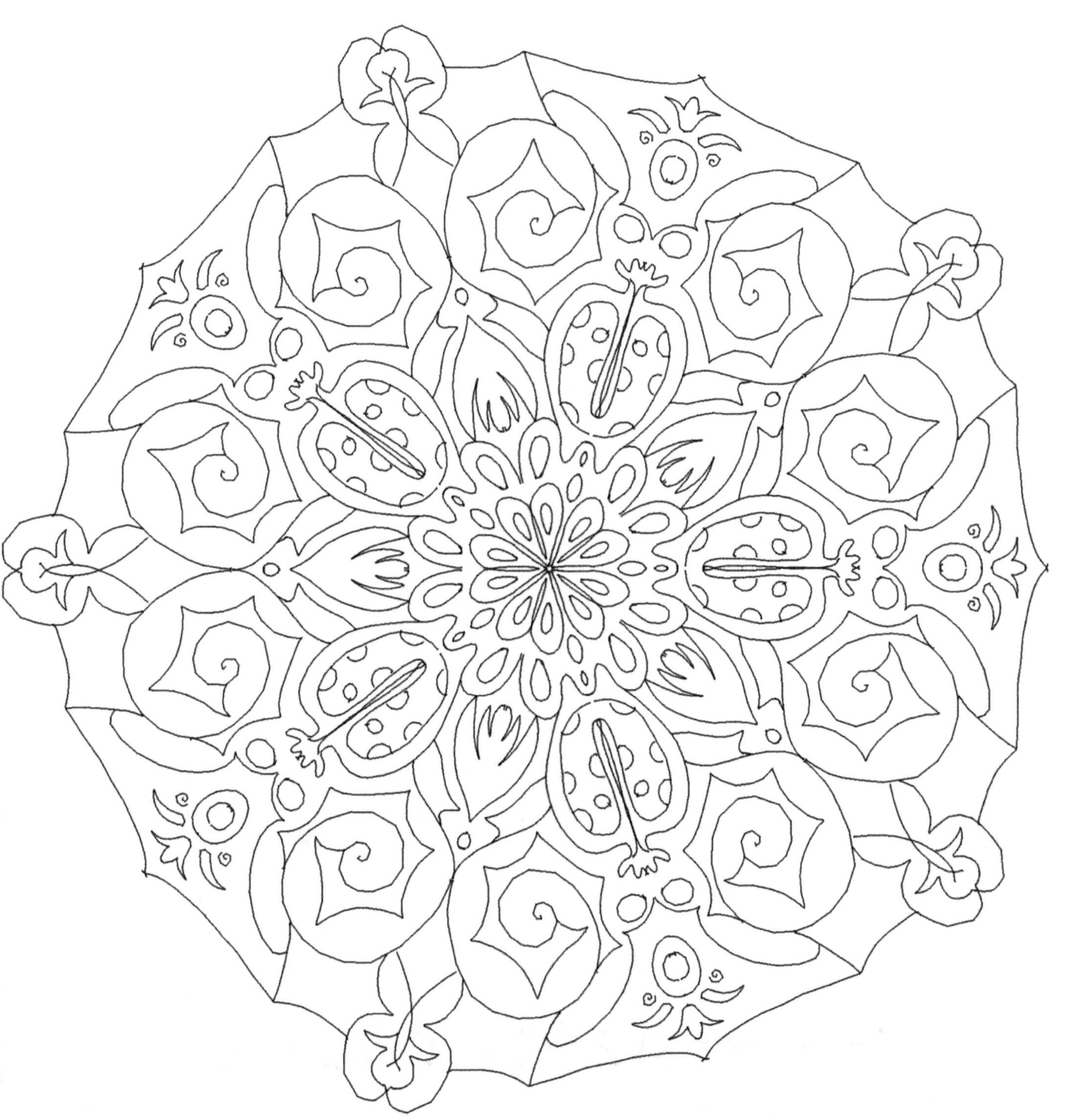

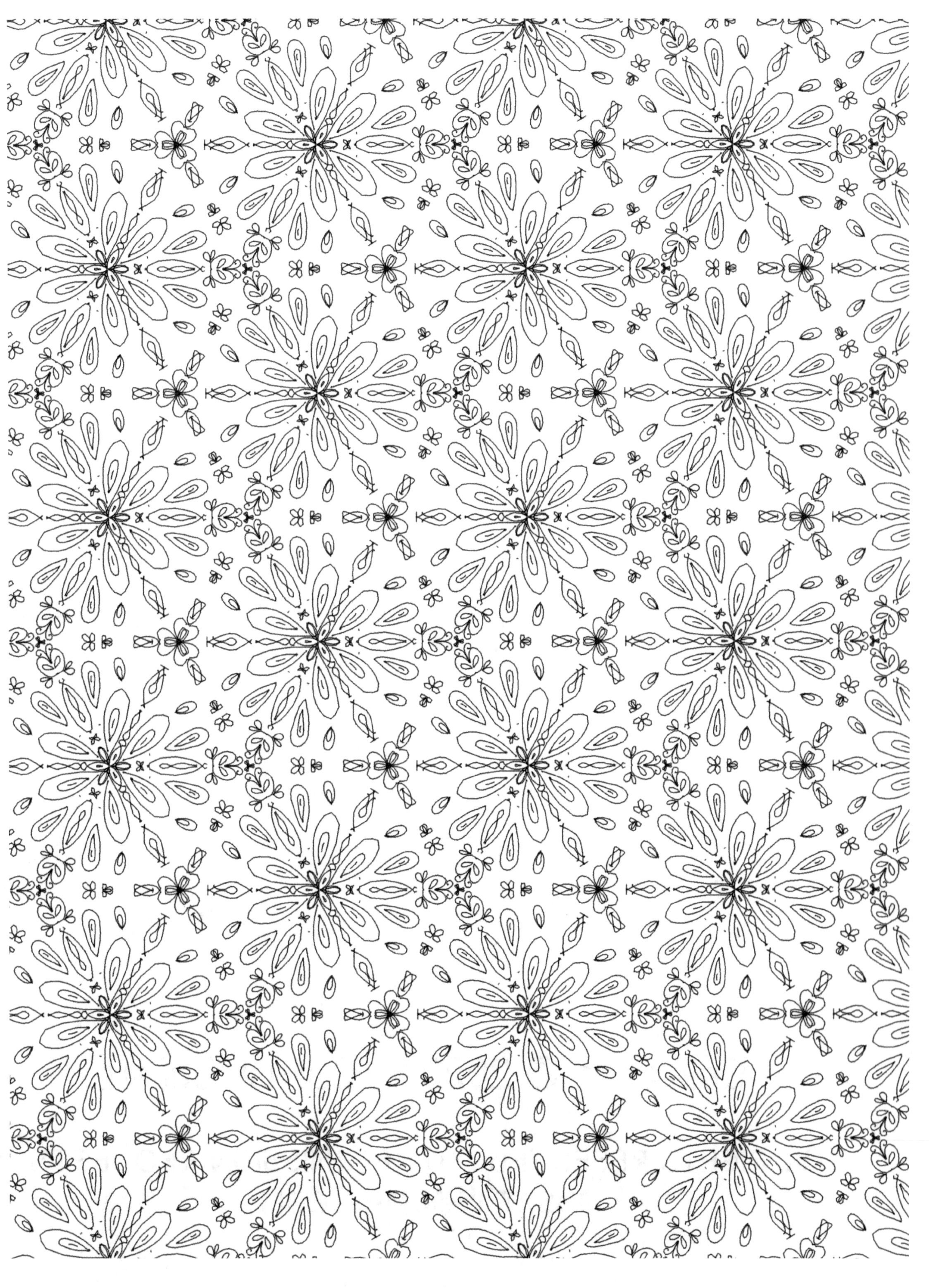

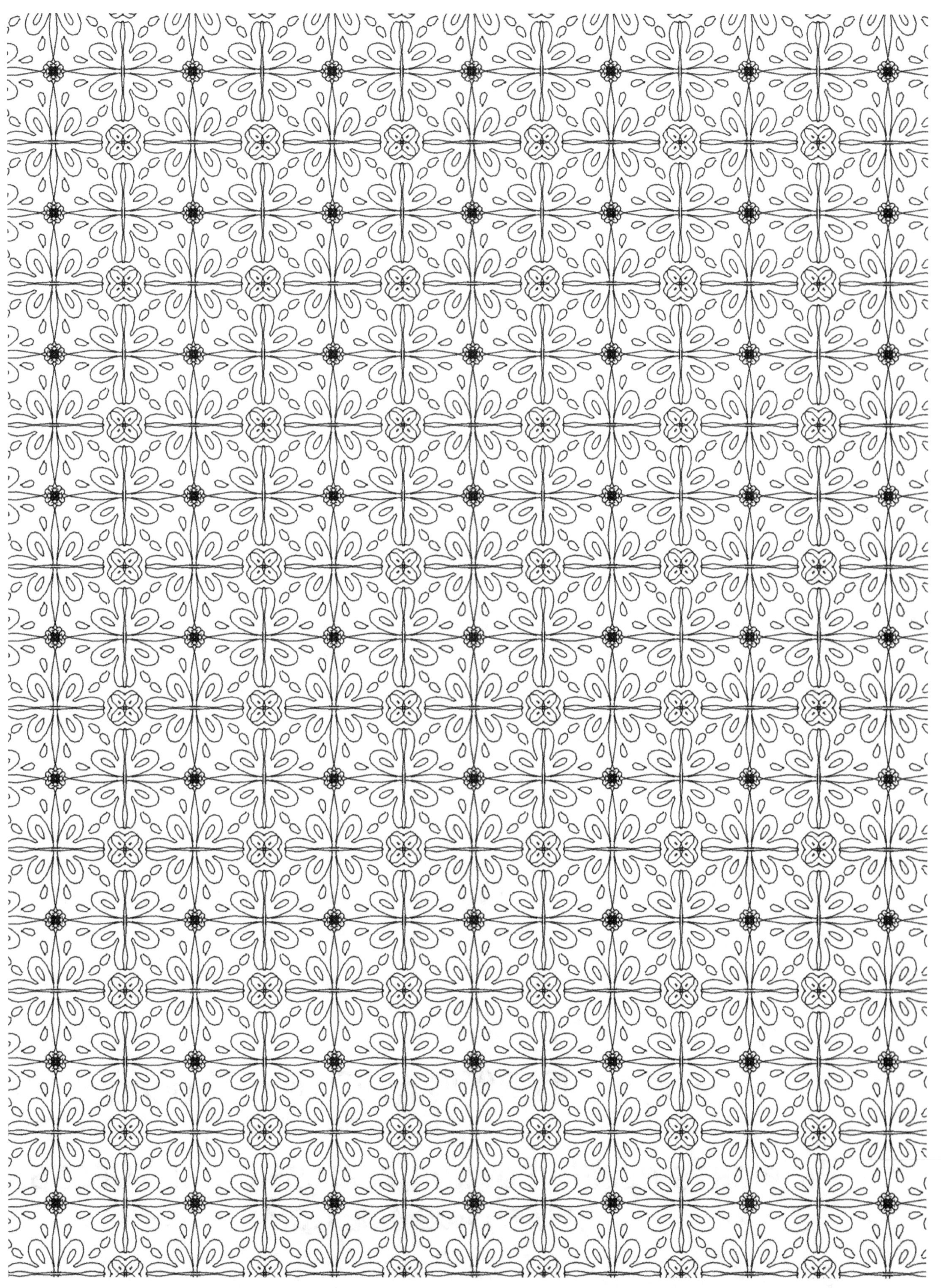

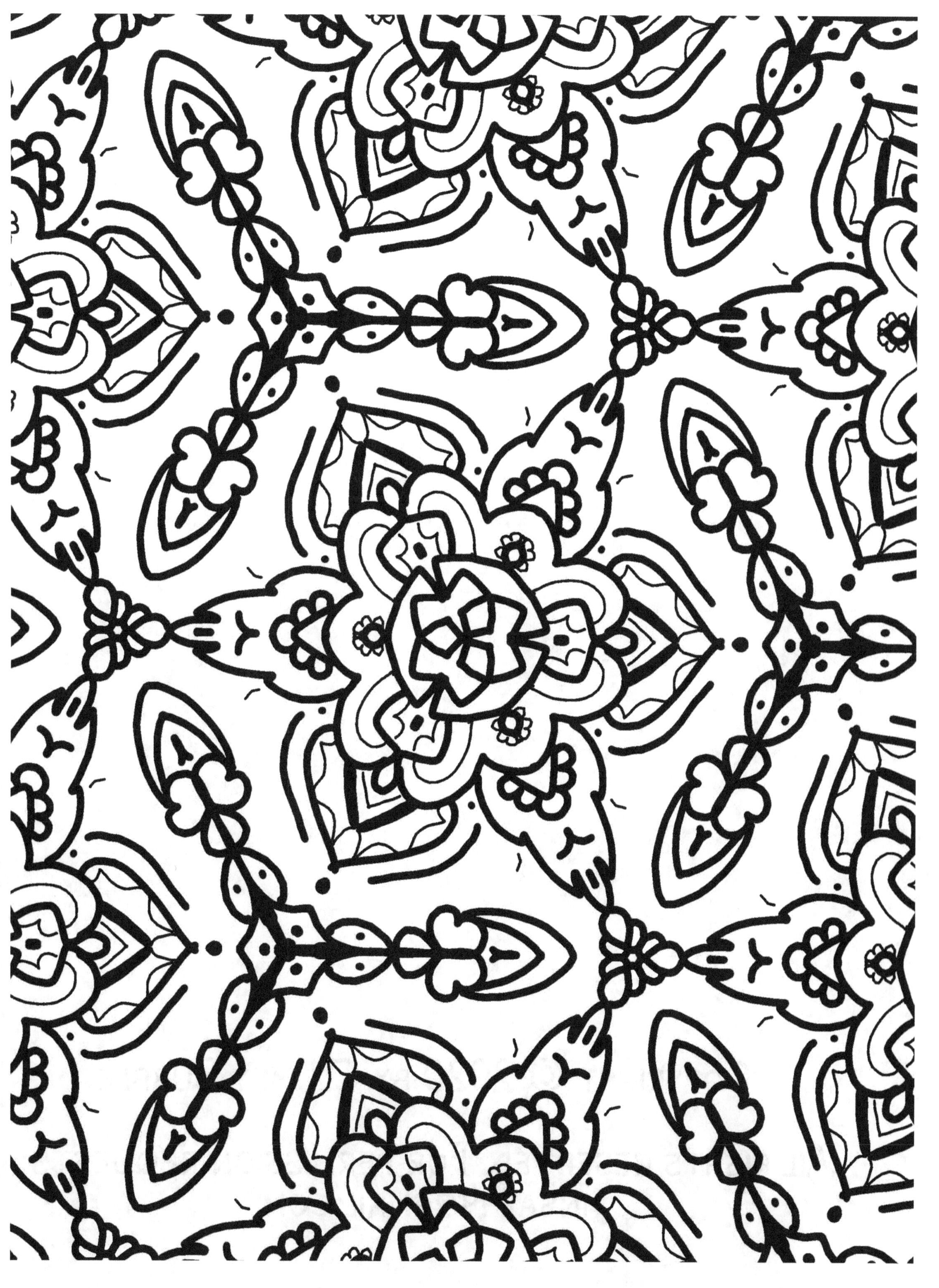

www.ingramcontent.com/pod-product-compliance
Lightning Source LLC
Chambersburg PA
CBHW081429250726
48654CB00013B/1883

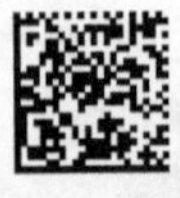